MORE PRAISE FOR

Bianca Stone

"Bianca Stone's poems are powerful, moving, and original. . . . In her poems, we're in the presence of a naked human voice, not concealing itself—or over-reaching to expose itself—which dives as deep as voices go."

—SHARON OLDS

"Bianca Stone's poetry has the glow of 21st-century enlightenment and lyric possession. Hilarious and powerful."

—MAJOR JACKSON

"I read the work of our most brilliant young poets to be reminded that it is still possible, despite everything, for our abused and decimated language to ring out the difficult truths of full-on awareness. The best of them, like Bianca Stone, do not settle for mere cleverness. They know it is not enough to be brilliant, that it is essential in poetry not only to report the miseries and blessings, but to transform them. . . . [I] believe she is going to the difficult places and writing these poems in service not just to herself, but to us all, so that we can go to them and together find a little hope."

—MATTHEW ZAPRUDER

"Stone's poems astutely and honestly address the longing and cost of human connections."

—*PUBLISHERS WEEKLY*

THE MÖBIUS
STRIP CLUB
OF GRIEF

THE MÖBIUS STRIP CLUB OF GRIEF

BIANCA STONE

 TIN HOUSE BOOKS / Portland, Oregon & Brooklyn, New York

Published by Tin House Books, Portland, Oregon, and Brooklyn, New York

Distributed by W. W. Norton & Company

Library of Congress Cataloging-in-Publication Data

Names: Stone, Bianca, author.
Title: The Möbius strip club of grief / by Bianca Stone.
Description: First U.S. edition. | Portland, OR : Tin House Books, 2018.
Identifiers: LCCN 2017034949 | ISBN 9781941040850 (pbk.)
Classification: LCC PS3619.T65643 A6 2018 | DDC 811/.6—dc23
LC record available at https://lccn.loc.gov/2017034949

First U.S. Edition 2018
Printed in the USA
Interior design by Jakob Vala

www.tinhouse.com

for
Grandma

Contents

II

Odin plucked out his eye in exchange for a drink
from Mimir's well of wisdom. He wanted to know
everything there is to know of the past and future. And so it was.
But the weight of wisdom made his face sour. Seeing everything
blown to shit. The gods with it. After that, he never ate again
and lived on a strict diet of alcoholic beverages
at the Möbius Strip Club of Grief.

I

Introduction

At the Möbius Strip Club of Grief, come on in, the ladies are
XXX! If you want the skinny ones we got skeletons cracking
round those poles. And over at the bar—there's Grandma, with
her breasts hanging at her stomach—gorgeous with a shook
manhattan, and murderous with a maxi pad. At the Möbius Strip
Club of Grief all the drinks are free. Grocery store rosé in gallon
bottles on every table. And the dead don't want your tips. They just
want you to listen to their poems. Don't do anything dangerous.
And call every once in a while. In fact, they tip *you* at the MSCOG.
With checks. With a sigh they'll throw one down at your feet—
We make it rain with checks.

Then the dead are sitting at the back of the club, dying further.
Sniffing. Shuffling into the bathrooms, holding their skin in their
hands, farting methane and sobbing across the stage with their last
meal—it's the raciest show in town. And ladies, there's *men* too,
hanging themselves on the bathroom doors and from the rafters,
totally naked, with their cocks in their hands, tears coming down
their faces. Ladies, you'll love how their feet smell. How their
bones protrude. How they leave no note.

Medieval

At the funeral they carried boom boxes on their shoulders,
blaring Chopin, swaggering over the snow in sync,
in all black, the cloth of penitents and matriarchs.

A hole is free to dig,
if you know how to ask men with the right tools.
Funerals need not break the bank.

Through the yard
like a procession of Danes and Duchesses from *Hamlet*,
all hired mourners from birth,
punters of rough gods,
women of the salons—

our funerals are like poker games
in the back room
at the Möbius Strip Club of Grief.
The stakes are high.
You have to have pneumonia to get in.
You have to cough and gurgle.
You have to have a cat on your lap.
And refuse to eat.

Last Words

After the funeral was out
the hors d'oeuvres came out.
Olives, pâté, sardines with soft bones and violent,
flushed organs—too much wine, slouched on a flowery chair—
aperitifs on the porch with the early moon—

I looked at the sky overhead where it said
in the white jet-stream cursive:
dying is awful.

And I lit my head on fire.
Danced a dance for the gods.
Mom pealed out, off down the mountain
like Mad Max
to sit alone in her house,
to play solitaire in the dark
because they'd turned off the lights again;
the pipes were frozen, the wood almost gone—
so solitaire on the floor beside the woodstove,

thinking
about abandonment
about love
about luck
about money—

like a winter songbird
it sang in her head all day:

Who will pay?
Who will pay?
Who will pay?

Lap Dance

I think everyone's glad I'm dead, said the stripper
with the caved-in face. Her fingers were bone and no
sinew. She flapped her arms at the two wrens
caught up in the rafters, staring down
on the empty dance hall. Chirps rained like sparks
from the electric saws in their hearts.
No one here is glad anyone is dead. But
there is a certain comfort in knowing
the dead can entertain us, if we wish. We line up
outside looking drowned, telling whoever comes
our way that we are falling very fast. And that
we are fine. The dead as wrinkled as jet streams
cutting across the room with glasses lost on their
heads, vitamins dissolving like milk
under tongues, hair still growing, crackling
out of their skulls in time-lapse loops—
and we file in, in ones and twos, clinging
to our tragedies, finding our favorite face,
and it looks back at us with indifference, contempt,
chill disappointment. *You never came much
when I was alive*, says one with red hair, lying
on her side, a Botticelli on the stage;
*and now you want a piece? $20 for five minutes;
I'll hold your hand in my own. I'll tell you
you were good to me.*

A Brief Topography of the MSCOG

I

Over the door there's the iconic ice-pick in a human heart. You
    have to show a scar to the bouncer to get in: the old suture
    holes, a common kneecap, the shy smile of a cesarean,
    spattering of long-gone acne—any scar will do. And you
    have to tell a story about your mother. Something she
    suffered through. But once you're in, you're in forever.

Then there's only the horizon, lush carpeting through
    cigarillo smoke, coats on hooks, worried aunts, croquet—
    grand as a yard sale, a ghost, her eyes like thumbs pointed
    down, her laugh like an almost perfect test score—

leave your inhibitions at the door. There is no room for modesty.
Your magnum opus will start

in the dim alcoves of grief.

II

Main dance room: frivolity, managed by a House Mom, who
    sits in a high swiveling chair, making sure no one breaks
    the rules of solitaire.

Lay me out on the floor and win me. I have nothing to give but my songs no one knows, on my album no one bought.

The DJ is the world, spinning and spinning.
On the loudspeakers it's Rubinstein at the piano, remixed
    with sick beats.

—and there's Grandma, half-blind, naked but for an open
    XL flannel and Birkenstocks. She peers out from behind
    the bar, squinting into the faces, trying to figure out who
    is ordering and what, her hand up behind her ear like a
    sail. *Don't let the cats out!* she screams, whenever someone
    comes in.

III

You want privacy with your dead?
Follow the nameless great-great-grandmothers through the
    screen doors.
Cross your hands over your chest like a coat of arms.
I will ravish you with songbirds.
You'll see angels bathing in dust.
Let there be something for you in one room or another.

And there are so many glow-in-the-dark galaxies to look upon.
Like you're all alone in your childhood bedroom,
but totally restored
in the adult entertainment industry's moral center.

IV

For the masochist, nothing quite hurts like the truth.

Farther in the cavernous club
where the bend in the strip fakes an edge,
I engrave my lunatic memorial:

                    I WAS HERE!

The dungeons of the mind, the most defeated cells,
wherein cruelty cums.

V

Let go and there is nothing
tethering you to the stake
that is always driven
into the soft center
of your vampiric world.

VI

The great cosmic cow gyrates her stomachs on stage. The
tall grasses sway at her knees. The people moan. The sun
sinks. The band wraps up with "Gloomy Sunday"—

Oh, Billie. Billie, do not leave us again—it never ends, it just
lies down and weeps, because it can't get ahold of anyone.
*HELLO?? Is anyone there?! Why aren't you answering your
phone??*—   lost in a magazine from 1998 about the
sky & telescopes. Let the moths land where they will.
Feel their powdery legs against your own. *Gloomy Sunday.
Gloo-my Sun-day.* Would the angels be mad if I thought
of joining you? Bright midnight moon, gloomy Sunday
through the glass ceiling—better yet, Mars: that raving
nipple, that red goddess who demands from the eaves to
be worshipped.

The Murder

I ground hemlock across your brow.
Shot you in the head.
Hid the gun in the river.
Looked inside the hole
of your temple—
looked inside
the oak tree's ragged scalp—
your bosom bubbles
and rots in the field.
I cast you out of your house
but your ghost lies down
in front of the stove
to weep,
to say you'd like a cup of instant coffee,
a piece of toast (that's all!),
and I bring it to you,
I poison you, Queen Gertrude,
in the center of a tournament,
pearl dropped
in a cup of rosé; lying down to die
again and again
in a tantrum and tempest—
I get the power saw.
Put the plastic tarp down.
Pass along your suicidal genes.

Your voluntary life in bed.
Window monarch—you
whom we fretted over
like superstitious servants
competing among your heavy furs and mantle—
How many grandmothers have I killed?
Some mornings I get up
and walk barefoot down the road
with my tin cup
to shake the tinsel loose from my bones,
to beg the strong winds
to touch me everywhere.
One sad epiphany after another
to survive this—
Oh, I survive this, I say to no one.
Dear, old flesh and blood,
these days I
would not recognize
your face
hidden in the ground
but for the sound of thunder,
the tremor of spring rain.

Client

I'm here, watching the dead spinning.
The dead are twerking and jiggling in my face.
The dead are goddesses, walking around the room
of wasted imbecilic dudes from Wall Street: the Living.
The living are so obliterated, they can barely see.
The dead are shaking our very foundations with their boobs.
And they're real—every part of them.
The dead are wild apples in your mouth.
They're all out there in the dark, working it.
Pissing in your belly button. Punching you in the jaw.
Forever.

Mama-san

The strippers tip the House Mom at the end of their shift.
With their life, their time, their sanity.
She sits at the center, conducting order.
She takes each aside to tell her she's brilliant.
(Too brilliant for anyone to appreciate.)

But the House Mom is trapped.
Owned by sorrow.

Up the back stairs it led them all each night: grief.
It tucked them in. It read itself aloud
in gilt fragments and tapestries fallen apart—

      and she made them say it back to her
      until they knew it by heart.

Hunter

Erotic dancing takes the place of Greek tragedy
just as the gladiatorial fights did in Rome—but it is a
    private dance
no one can touch or see. A feeling every day I enter and close
a curtain behind. Sitting alone with it,
looking at it through a tiny hole,
something lithe and naked, shaking in the spotlight
beyond which I can never reach—

suffering cannot do what it did for Christ.
We do not get to go home afterward, cannot be
imagined into the arms of the absent father. See how
I do not rise up or shift the stone, do not
inspire a nation—I sit at the bar
consuming fried food. I put $5 into a machine
and shoot bucks with a long green rifle,
not speaking, not calling out anyone's name,
just me and the deer
grazing in a digital clearing of the wood.

I can't tell anymore for whom I grieve.
Something bigger
and more catastrophic has died
but died out of necessity—something that thought itself
into *indispensability*
something burst from every atom
outward, like autumn fireworks over the lake
and now
I'm just recording its scream and glitter-down,
just making a serial
from its fantastical, dazzling demise—
I can't tell anymore whether I am grieving *you* particularly
or I simply find life and death erroneous—this
big expired grief
                    like limbs people deny ownership of, find
in their beds and throw on the floor, only to be told
          again and again, when the
whole body is thrown with it—that it is

attached,

     it is theirs, that they were
born with it.

All the Single Mothers

A Möbius strip has a surface
with only one side,
only one boundary—it cannot be
its own mirror image.
Just as a family is
        deformed by symmetry—
our favorite kind of beautiful here.

When the men came
they came in Doppler shifts,
frequency fading
the moment they passed by.
The rest of their voices' pitch
was relative to the air—
and when we were born
we listened to them fade away
as if they were never there.

Honeybee

When the male enters a female honeybee
and manages climax

his genitals explode
       and break off his body.
It is the most dedicated orgasm in the universe.
His penis stoppers her
       like Ali Baba's boulder at the entryway to a cave of treasure:

she's sealed with a spell.

       Having sired their tragic progeny
and prevented another from entering her

the male bleeds out
       and dies in the grass. This really happens.
So it is at the Möbius Strip Club of Grief.

Off-hours, the dead wait at the center of the room, sitting
       backward in chairs,
lounging in nipple-tassels,
reading goodbye letters that'd been tucked into their caskets.

The disco ball in the center of the room
is like a flamboyant, pockmarked moon
        spinning silver acne over the dancing dead.

The pollen is aching.

When it's time,

the competition is fierce here in the air.
25,000 males assemble and compete for a single, deadly orgasm.

Progeny is everything here.

        Our motto is:
        I'd rather be dead than share you with another.

Emily Dickinson

Some nights she comes to act as courier,
midwife to our own skills.
Emily, come like a UFO to implant her genius in us.
Our Queen Mab, condemned to be the only woman mentioned
in the lyric omnibuses of her epoch;
easy scapegoat of men's centuries,
she stood in for all women.
So now, of course, she comes to blow off steam
in the privacy of the green room.
All those living years she walked from yard to yard,
gardens flourished in opium poppies;
went out at night to see the owls and wed her genius.
She applied her passion like a hot iron sword.
And no one can take off her clothes, ever—she comes
and her language takes them off of *us*,
not piece by piece, not fumbling buttons,
but all at once in a single shot,
her tiny poems like grenades that fit in the hand.
And we here bask in the debris,
stripped down to our private parts,
the snow white of the bone, the authentic corpse in heat.
The absolute original.

Math

I used to sit in the bathroom stall at school
and weep
about math—

But it is possible here
in the nightclub of naked, spiritual wellness
for those who never got it before.

It's a kind of vanity
you can commiserate over with strippers
who fall under the mathematical term *homeomorphism*,

which means if you stretch and stretch
you can make a version of yourself out of them;
their topological space is equal to our own,
just as a doughnut and coffee mug are equal.

Do you understand?
There's so much to learn.

An even number of nipples
swaying in the strobe-lit main thoroughfare;

the murmuring of understanding,
ah-ha moments of orgasm
like reaching an original state of consciousness,

that brief moment of freedom
from the memory of your education.

The strippers will bend over you
at your tiny round table

breathing cream-and-sugar coffee into your ear
asking you if you need anything;

rethink this,
check your math—

    I'm here for you, the ancestry says

placing a gold star on your cheek

where an F should be.

I Am Unfaithful to You with My Genius

I

There are no time periods this does not extend to. It's *a priori*, omnipotent, a salon of the underworld, full of noblesse with their vast sprinkling of literature and philosophy. Women of letters who cast about in their intimate coteries the halo of their own genius. Women who go at it with trumpet & lyre, not flute, nor harp; and men in wild metamorphoses—*to hell with Time*, they say, wandering in and out of the confines of your little world, hoping upon hope to pull you out of the past and into the gorgeous, death-rattling moment.

II

When we die we strip—wash, harden, burn, urinate, bloat, grind into a fine powder, into a paste, spread on the endless paper cuts of our descendants. There is no room for modesty in this vague realism. But hours after the moment of death the body below the head looks creepily good—have you seen the dead stripped? Death's last-minute cosmetic surgery, the skin taut from gravity, confined in beauty for one last hurrah.

Then we lie naked before nature and let her ravish us—undoing everything.

III

Ladies, enjoy the pleasures of your own mind! The creative
woman in this living patriarchy wants to be both object
and subject of creation. *Blow up your television, love me
instead*, my genius says to me.

IV

"Inspire, but do not write," said Lebrun in his poem "To lovely
ladies who want to be poets":

> *The Gods created you for love*
> *Love would look with anger burning*
> *To see you waste your night on poems.*

V

"I feel a little worthless with your pregnancy," my husband
said, coming home after Magic: The Gathering; my
husband, full of whiskey, beside me on the bed, began
describing his realization that men created a patriarchal
society in order to be indispensable. Simple scientific
preparation of a sperm bank could make them totally
valueless. When men saw what women could create,

they freaked out. And from that crippling feeling of
inadequacy at being unable to bear children, men went on
to prove that they were the best creators. I thought this
was a very wise observation, and I agreed.

"Inspire, but do not write," said Lebrun to women, hoping
that women would not notice that we were already *built*
to write; born, ourselves, a loaded gun, ready to produce
language and meaning and sense.

VI

True, women like to inspire; they are not greedy about it.
They temper their minds in order to give. It's a delicate
blending of many gifts, not the supremacy of a single one.
"It implies taste and versatility, with fine discrimination,
and the tact to sink one's personality as well as to call out
the best in others."

VII

Ponce Denis Écouchard Lebrun, the French Reign of
Terror's official poet. And in his private life, he wielded
his particular horrors, beating his wife in his rages. His
own mother and sister helped her escape. Critics agree,
a few fine strophes, but not one good ode. Drink to his
death. To his failures.

VIII

But then, perhaps it is I who eat the bread of a different failure.
Never a flower. Never the beautiful white heifer who
wandered among the black and green seaweeds, wondering
what the hell had happened. I was never hidden by Jove.
I cannot write about beauty, which rankles and drives no
chariot of fire before me, but instead lies out on a slab of
wood in the rain, and stays neither wet nor dry.

And my education: I did not learn but as I went, plodding,
    inelegant through institutions, like my women before me.
    When I sit down to write I feel unfaithful, to someone,
    to something. Why should I do one thing over another?
    Like when pulling a wildflower out of a patch of flowers,
    my flesh cannot determine, anymore, why this and not
    that. I burn everything down so it might grow back. I love
    the sexual dichotomy of myths and legends. I watch the
    usurped tremble with lust from a tiny dais in the moment.
    And it feels almost good to glower through my life. To
    listen to the old guard at the podiums in small, New
    England towns, speaking of women at cocktail parties,
    "who dress to be seen" but are quickly undressed by men's
    eyes (the joke's on them!). It feels good to nod in the back
    row, knowingly, as Anne Geneviève de Bourbon, Duchesse
    de Longueville, no doubt did at the Hôtel de Rambouillet,
    yawning over the scholarly discourse of Balzac, enduring
    the endless disputes over rival sonnets. Long, tiresome,
    beautiful poems—I can listen, and nod. I can live. While
    the female gnostic god locates herself in the self, potential
    recognized in a flash in the mirror as in a horror movie—
    aboriginal self, entity anonymous—

The neon yet taupe and pale-purple sunset sets in your loins.
    The god indoors knits, patient as a Whistler, while outside
    the satanic establishment edits your skin like a bruise

IX

You, your husband, your children—whose genius am I among?
  You plucked the pencil from your lover's hand. I'm sitting
  in his old office in your spinning wooden chair, and now
  you both are dead. He hanged himself, and you died of
  pneumonia. Out in the backyard, farthest from the brook,
  you lie like a vampire in your box. If I could go out and dig
  you up and rub your leathered face with mine, I would—
  like Antigone I would ruin myself for you. Your skull is so
  close. Your body so near—I could stand on it like a stage.
  Bow, and let the lights fade. Raised like a poem is raised—
  far too undone; a single wolf, stalker, woman's external
  demon of genius—mad genius—the best kind of person to
  suffer for
raised up at the feet; and I know no other—
"Fall at the feet of this sex to whom you owe your mother."

II

The natural sublime is intimately bound up with place, often occasioned by a beauty that is painful, and entangled with the grief we experience at the overwhelming losses we have inflicted on the natural world and one another in relation to it.

—Bonnie Mann, *Women's Liberation and the Sublime: Feminism, Postmodernism, Environment*

Making Applesauce with My Dead Grandmother

I dig her up and plop her down in a wicker chair.
She's going to make applesauce and I'm going to get drunk.
She's cutting worms out of the small green apples from the
    backyard
and I'm opening a bottle. It erects like a tower
in the city of my mouth.

The way she makes applesauce, it has ragged
strips of skin and spreads thickly over toast.
It's famous; eating it is as close to God as I'm going to get,
but I don't tell her. There's a dishtowel wrapped around her head
to keep her jaw from falling slack—

Everything hurts.
But I don't tell her that either. I have to stand at the call box
and see what words I can squeeze in. I'm getting worried.
If I dig her up and put her down in the wicker chair
I'd better be ready for the rest of the family

to make a fuss about it. I'd better bring her back right.
The whole house smells of cinnamon and dust.
We don't speak. She's piling up the worms, half-alive
in a silver bowl, she's throwing them back into the ground
right where her body should be.

How Not

Be completely dispassionate about the theoretical five stages.
This is an old death, but it's your death. Complete the stages
in blurring fits of inebriation. Eat everything in sight. Fight
with your mother. Marry Ben in the woods. Fly across
the country. Stand in the street with the raging legless
angel. Hold a brick wall very close to your face.

Interior Design

How fabulous that humans are able to decorate from their
    minds. In a sense, they splatter their brains on the walls,
    translate texture from the head onto objects; carve into
    the very tusk, chisel onto the veranda, sew into quilts and
    lay them over the bodies of guests.

And what joy I get from that. From *décor*. From personal flair.
(Just look at the detail! Velvet. Chintz. Oak. Mint-condition.
    Patina. Hand-stitched . . .)
Even an absence of objects reflects a certain taste.

*

I hold court all day on my own intellectual shortcomings.
It doesn't matter anymore. I'm led through hallways
into blue and gold vestiges
of the old rue Saint-Thomas-du-Louvre
and the historic apartments that adorned it.
I enter the rank beauty of my women's homes:
the familiar minute details of hoarding; draperies
in mixed scenes of toile, Venetian lamps, boxes, endless mail,
vases large enough to hold a child, filled with flowers
on their last legs, scattering the perfume of almost-decay.

I rendezvous in the living room with Mom.
I feel like your rejection slips, collated in a folder. Outdated
 science magazine
of inaccurate information—
I would love to "move on." But I carry you around like a scar,
forgetting sometimes that it is even there
until I follow a stranger's eye to it during a handshake.

*

My father-in-law keeps his wife's ashes in a tiny silver golf
 bag around his neck.
His favorite word is *nice*. When the service is "nice," the
 world makes sense. He wants the world to do a nice job.
If I could, I'd have kept a nice bone from your hand,
a notch of your middle finger, or a long clavicle; your whole
 skull . . .
But I would not have kept ashes.

Ashes remind me of my childhood,
shoveling them into a metal bucket from the woodstove
and sneaking them across the road
to dump in the cow field—Mom crying out for a load of wood
on my way back in—to me, ashes are too
anonymous.

*

Ah, so posh, so tasteful in grief. Some aesthetic leftover from
    the Greeks
mingled with the late booty of colonialism.
It fills me with a sense of leadership just being among the
    collected, the amassed,
the eccentric.

If I were to make a banner for my House it might be
a gray owl with its talons outstretched,
a 1989 Toyota broken down on the side of the road,
a blue jay in the center field of black wheat stalks,
a woman's silhouette at the center of a pentagram—
my flag would be so Metal, so Hardcore,
with a touch of *the feminine, beaux esprits.*
Something of gallantry,
integrity, and science, all wrapped up in one emblematic clutch—

Nothing was ever "nice" in my family.
They bear an intensity that allows
only for extremes:

     It's always been either "You're a *genius!*"
Or "You're a Hitler."

Flight

Someone told Mom it takes six months to realize
   someone is no longer on the planet.
On a commuter plane from Portland to Seattle
it was exactly six months later,
   on the tiniest plane in the world.
I broke out in hives
   like a nun blushing all over for God—
a sweeping bloodshot victory
   eating everything
while the other feelings starve—

the plane shook, and I grabbed the leg of the woman sitting
  next to me.
   She looked taken aback, then returned to her real-
  estate magazine
without a word
    while silvery tears rolled down my face onto a
  book called *VALIS*,
   which was open onto the first page.

Strangers shake in the breeze of my cannonball looks—

out the round window I could see below me
Washington State
and the same repeated genus of spruce.

I happened to have a pamphlet with me, *Important Trees of
Eastern Forests*
from 1968. I opened to the swamp cottonwood, which grows
in Mom's front yard.

Whenever I fly
I feel that I'm being forced to accept my own death.
And now, simultaneously,
I was being forced to accept the death of someone else.

I knew that once I accepted it, I could accept the free sample
of local Washington beer in plastic party cups the
flight attendants came around with
like a blessed and bitter medicinal syrup
pulled from a prehistoric wheat.

The Reading

It's her birthday the day I read with Mark at the bookstore in Iowa.
I'm terribly hungover. I tell Mark to read his long poem
about the crushing, overpowering beauty and intellect of women.
I've eaten myself into an enormous oblivion.
My whole face screams LACK OF RESTRAINT.

I take my time at the reading. Let each word leap
and plummet, and lie down in front of me.
It's like there're no punches to pull. Like there's no weather.

It's like I'm reading in a vacuum of my own dehydrated vileness.
It's like I'm reversing; blowing everything back into a joint
and missing phone calls. It's like I'm standing in a fresco,
powdering myself in a cloud of dried lime.
It's like she's hiding in a sleeping bag on the front porch,
and I have to climb in with her and tell her she's dead.

Self-Destruction Sequence

Regarding falling asleep
waiting for my group to be called
to enter the tunnel
that would have taken me
to 26D—
I nodded off, the plane left
without me
in my neck pillow
like someone in a hospital bed
completely unaware, waiting to be fixed,
indifferent to everything.
And perhaps what makes us miss things
is that once in a while
we want to stop getting what we're paying for,
a small Dostoyevskian mutiny
like buying a clear plastic box of salad
that tastes old and poisonous
then throwing the whole thing in the trash.
Our lives are a series of
debts and payoffs that feel barely
tolerable. And anyway
whenever I walk across the sky
to stand in line for the bathroom
I think, finally,
I am just like a ghost

walking over the world
trying to distract myself
from boredom
and hysteria. It's a kind of
holy moment
that unfills
anger.

Stenographer

Never mind where I was.
It was like 4:45
and the bartender had great hair.
I was breaking apart, taking notes.
I had to stand at the very end
and wave at her for my drinks.
Reading *VALIS*
by candlelight
I felt like Buddha
losing my mind in a back room
or stenographer women
who type in courthouses
while everyone rages around them—it's a life
of listening to and typing
sentences
said by other people,
and right now
it seems like no one in this place
wants to mean anything,
which is okay.
In my head I'm saying
in 300+ words,
I'm afraid and very hopeful.

Elegy with a Swear Word

A planet may hide hundreds of planets.
My planet hides in the hands
of physicists.
My heart, stoned and eating everything.
Subspace signature
telling another signature
we understand nothing.
Ghosts in the vocabulary.
Sorrow is a mansion.
A burning bush in the middle
of a transcendental bar fight.
The known universe
is saying *Fuck*, softly
into the unknown universe.
It's a very long winter.
I can't remember anyone's name
or whether I finished my beer.

Cliff Elegy

for Emily P.

When you're falling off the precipice
look up at the finger of the cliff you just stood on
where there's a lemur waving his tiny black hand
getting tinier and tinier; look beside you, when
you're falling, like Alice, and see there's a white
horse breaking your mind
in a good way. There's a whole set of glasses
filled up with different drinks, and someone
who wants to get very close to your cheek
with his cheek, and tell you something loving:
That you came with milkshakes in the evenings
and fed the cat. That this is only partway down.
The air is thin but there are so many particles
in it. And there're chairs to sit on, and tables
to match. Being partway you can see everything,
the up and the down, the sideways and the
inwardways. You have all this time. All
this time to still fall for him.

The Fates

I cracked open my skull and out flew Mom.
She alighted on the rafters, electric in a massive chamber.
She has abilities accessed by latent genes.
Quietly terrible powers come
with great responsibility—which
you don't have to honor—either way you still
have the power;
a few lives to fuck up, to
wreck or save—
wind chimes won't let go of me.
I ring whenever I move.
I feel like the *Titanic* sailing straight
into the liquor store on St. Marks at Franklin.
I'm watching a TV show
about supernatural detective brothers
who travel back and forth across the United States
avenging their parents' deaths
until they can't remember anymore why or how the parents died—
in general
the need to kill demons and vampires
overtakes the brothers' need
to remember anything.
And who can blame them?
Every night in the hotel the two talk indirectly about their feelings—
manly men, massive in sex appeal, drinking

and killing and talking.
In this episode the Services of Fate are no longer required in
    the human world.
Thus, everything in the future is affected.
In this reality
I know my brother is living near me,
so close
I can wave from my window
into his.
He's telling me he's writing
about the way
the face disappears.

Dear Sister

for Hillery

> Dear Sister—After you went, a low wind warbled
> through the house like a spacious bird, making it
> high but lonely. When you had gone the love came.
> I supposed it would. The supper of the heart is when
> the guest has gone.
>
> —Emily Dickinson to Mrs. J. G. Holland

I

In fear of death we lose out on life. We stuff an owl with
    arsenic and leave it totally perfectly not alive in the study,
    like something coveted privately by Calypso, like the
    greatest line ever written, embalmed with iron, staring
    down at us from the filing cabinet, never read aloud.
    What makes us despair is the impermanence of beauty.
    Until Nothing is beautiful we despair.

II

My sister and I write back and forth about Mom. "Have you
    talked to Mom?" "No. Did you?" Mom is deep into Jewish
    mysticism. She sits in the second row of an Elie Wiesel
    talk at the 92nd Street Y. She makes elaborate notes and
    drawings in her journal. The row is empty except for her.
    "I had the whole front row!" she says. "It was bizarre. No

one would sit by me!" Mom dreams about Grandma. My
sister scrubs the table each morning before the children
get up. She feels the insects of the mind against her
skin. They lay their precious eggs in her, they climb her,
sac, follicle, and feeler. She papers the cupboards with
instructions on how to feed everyone. She writes about the
body confused, lost, undone. Writes about the currency of
children. Her neurons fire and smolder—she wants to be
loved right. She arranges the weekend away.

And of those ancient peoples just discovered, who
    constructed totem poles displaying wolves and demons—
    where are their bones now? Or the genes, unraveled and
    rewired, stretched like taffy—do they mean eternity?

III

Truth is always getting closer, vanishing everything possessed
    by inertia. When Grandma died her forehead perspired and
    a sickly sweet odor filled us, like the calm urine of infants.

              In my mind,
                in my mind, in my mind for days
after there was only a nail when I closed my eyes.
A new, straight nail. Upright, unpounded.

In my mind for days after: Antigone.

Antigone, whose portrait I was drawing as a horse that
    couldn't be tamed.
A wild horse with goggles who disrupted dinner parties.
    Antigone, who couldn't stand the idea of her brother's
    body out there with the wolves, and dug a grave with a
    shovel and her bare hands, all alone in the creepy night.

Antigone, whose sister wanted to row out into the darkest
    water with her—

wicker and stovepipe, fluid and skin—the body, not assumed,
    lies still in the ground—

love's gross duties—the body is a continuous bloom with a
    terrible fragrance.
There is nothing to stop you from taking it into your arms,
    telling it
it is good.

The Gang Elegy

It lies deep in my psyche.
Like neuroscience or whatever.
Like all my old Archie comics.
Like wind, fooling around with me.
Like sweet liquid from a sherry glass.
It lounges in my old punk shadow.

Blue Jays

I

Great men will tell us how they rose from nothing.
But Mom's a teenage heartbreak, deadly bright
blue jay in the snow, her vivid black beak queenly
inside a flush of blue. She's a prologue the size
of a whole book—she's real poppies
that will make you sleep—so much
motherland in her, I'm adrift in an age
of not giving up.

A fog lies over everything when she's upset.
People used to live in the attic, ones
who snuck down when we went out, to use the toilet and
    steal the spoons—
Nothing's up there! I said. Though
I had no idea—
        Mom writing down license plates while
we sat in the car outside the bakery
eating croissants—so many similarities in numbers. It can be
beauty to see.

In the fields of Illinois
Mom danced topless for the soldiers headed to war.
        "Probably be the last thing I see before I hit the shit,"
one man told her.

And

                Blue, here is a shell for you—

Text messages like leaves on a river
moving swiftly toward
the vast sea of misunderstanding.

Wouldn't it be nice to live more than one lifetime?
I want to be something else for a little while.
I'm the village idiot savant standing at an empty
wishing well, lighting a joint and getting paranoid,
telling one yarn after another to anyone who will listen.

Mom was always changing her name, asking to be called
something different. One day she went into the courthouse
and wrote the name *Blue Jay* on a blank line; the jay that will
        gather all the other jays
when a dead one is found, assemble the others to grieve—

the name's still on her license like a hieroglyph;
unusable, dust long ago gathered upon—

Who are you? she asked one night
        standing beside the four-poster bed in the dark—*who*
    ARE you?

You know me, don't you?
I can't
        remember all the words
to that one lullaby; I've grown backward and down.

No room to sit,
        no private place to plunder,
tall as the tallest French bisque doll in the house

but I barely fit into these collections of genius,
never shipped
into society, only stockpiled
for the end of the world.

I bought her *Mind Whispering.* And *The Motivation Manifesto.*

I bought *The Life-Changing Magic of Tidying Up*, left it
    among the Jewish-mysticism books

and later it appeared in a pile by the front door.
"Take your self-help book back with you," she said,
filling a glass with ice and Diet Pepsi
like an ocean wave foaming over stones—

My holes were empty like a cup,
In every hole sea came up
Till it could come no more.

II

Enough, enough!
Now I start my own cult.

I lead
        some commune of rapture

for these wounds. But it does no good.

Instead everyone commits
great big acts of suicide together in my head.

III

Back during our brief Mormon days
Mom wouldn't let us go to temple
out in Utah and baptize the dead.

"But I can baptize your father," I insisted,
who'd hanged himself all those years ago.
"He was a Jew," Mom said. "He doesn't want
to be baptized into the three Mormon heavens."

And that was that.

Soon after, we stopped attending, and really
I was glad. I didn't want to baptize the dead so much
as get into a swimming pool and be held down
by a gentle hand of the priesthood.

"Your brother got too serious," Mom said, smoking
in the car in her wool jacket with the elastic loops for
    shotgun shells
and the flannel insert and loose M&M's in the pockets
(I loved her in that coat). "He said I was sinning for drinking
    coffee."

Nowadays it's, like, two cocktails and my endorphins are spent,
with a big shiny silver dollar, and I'm an old doll
that talks gibberish   when pulled apart.

I rush home
with my golden ticket of shit
        and pass out in the empty tub.

IV

No one will talk about her father's death in a new way.
It came out quietly that he liked to wear women's clothes—
tenderly, Mom tells me this—

 His unfinished dissertation that crumbles in my hands;
his poems from 1943, student soldier ballads done
with quivering golf pencils—

I'm so alone, I'm so alone without you
my darling—

Oh, I wish him on her!
Wish him on her to be loved!

To be loved properly by a father probably feels great.
Like winning a medal.

V

There's so much joy in this poem. I'm trying
to convey how much
I love my mother, the way I love birds.

The blue jay always
is the biggest bird around the bird feeder—makes
strange, loud songs,
a little aggressive, but gorgeous, known
for its intelligence and complex social systems
with tight family bonds, a biblical fondness for acorns,
spreading oak trees into existence
after the last glacial period.

VI

I don't want you to think I'm stealing these things
from your life. What is stealing when it's your own
body parts, manufactured and passed down?
Like a cameo brooch looking out across the hills
of the breastbone, layers of skin and fat,
important bacteria from the vagina,
bracelets rattling on an arm—
sometimes it's just the way the hair falls
off the skull, or the glass eyeball
that rolls around at night
on the floor of the cave in your dark mind.

VII

What of those immigrant Lithuanian Jews
who all married goyim with red hair?
After his wife died, Great-Uncle Jack, your father's brother,
wouldn't throw anything out,
filling his house with newspapers and *New Yorkers*—
but Oh his seders in Baltimore we screamed through, so happy,
the delicious sounds of his muttering Hebrew—

can we go back?
This poem is for you, hoarders of my blood.

VIII

The gentle climate of mothers that shakes the White House
      —and other times drives you
insane with silence. The silent treatment,

the defining absence of noise,
like an expanding stain, damp and long,
face of need,
      need more forceful the longer it gets—typing out
sad sentences like a telegram into the hands
of the wrong person—
my sweet placemat I place at my table each day.

When I sit down with a blue jay, the seeds fall out of my mouth.

Do you know the game?
The game is leading you out of the dark
and then you long to go back in—
or blowing into your hands to make a fire
or building something on top of another thing
and one is more fragile than the other.

IX

My sister and I
are stars in our own reality show
that no one watches but us
    ("Has Mom responded?")

spread out in omnipotent banter
waiting for our relationship with Mom to *really begin*

To be loved without a fight
with a calm center—not
passing a mood around like a screaming infant

this black-market DVD collection
that cannot be watched
except when the moon is waning
and no one paid the electric bill
and they're threatening to take the house
and the hostile cats are locked in the bathroom—

and then
you can't look away
for anything.

X

Watch me loving you forever, Mom, on this strip of land
we call grief—but it is only life!

Do you know the game?
The game is called Being Unhappy, Just in Case.
or Gratitude as a Weakness.

And we play sometimes when there is nothing else to do.

XI

Thunder & lightning outside turns to reverence.

Realizing your parents are just human
is a large part of mature development.
                Some people never get there,
and being there is evanescent.

XII

Suddenly this need for honey in everything; seasickness bands
on my wrists remind me of my old perversity,
blackout incisions on the skin, an injury, open-eye-shaped,
   woman's-shame-shaped—

Get up out of the internet, Lawnmower Man!
I'm concerned about the way we keep looking
for something to ease the pain—
I'm not yet like a Navy SEAL, the way they love it
when things are miserable.
Living is enduring painful situations.
But Living, certainly, is *not* Reality,
which, as we know, is such a lark, Mom, don't we?

*

An exotic bird comes to solve herself in the backcloth of ash
   trees.

I dream again I am so articulate
with my vicious insults.

XIII

Grief for the living will ruin your appetite.
How much do bird species watch other bird species?

"Like blue terriers"
        Emily Dickinson said of the jays.

Mimicking the cry of a hawk—

the Old World jay who will intuit his female's state of mind
and find her the food she most desires—
the jay will watch closely and keep track.

Being loved depends upon it.

I've been watching you from this damp branch,
the wily sun
        across your sullen face, your bones among your features,
your mouth curled, beautiful, angry—a child's lips

that whorl on a word.

Your sisters—from the same Edenic womb,
who crossed the red sea of the maddening mother—
cannot reason together.

Just jays scattered across the country surviving on
the delicacy of larvae.
The seed feeder swinging like a crystal pendulum saying

     Yes—

"I miss you in the world," I said to you yesterday, sitting on
    the couch while
you threaded tiny Italian imported beads onto string
in your manor of magnificent lamps
illuminating;

the veil Dickinson noticed
       hovering over the imperfectly beheld face
fluttering
with your out-breath of cigarette smoke,

an old wound reddening around you,
your genius trapped like a moth on the screened-in porch of
    your pain—

waiting in your house for a miracle. Oh,
       Mother—it will never come without your consent.

*

Mothers are all I have ever known.
And my loyalty, never amassed enough. My labyrinth. My
     confusion of jays, my
"cacophonous aggregation." University of humor
and ingenious abilities
I come back to again and again, to hang out and argue
—dearest playmate, won't you come out
and play with me?

"I'm dead and in hell. I've known that for years," you say.
And I step quietly back into the night.

Ones Who Got Away with It

I still fantasize I can do something about it.
That girl in the outpatient-care facility for teenagers
confided to me that she sneaked out to see a guy
at his frat party, and he *shared* her with his three friends,
to have a taste after he was done. "Is it supposed
to hurt so much?" she whispered to me. "I mean,
for this long *after?*" She was bulimic, and we both
hated our mothers. The next day I said, *We should*
tell someone. And she said, "I've talked it over
with my best friend. She says
I should be proud of it." She was thirteen
and I, sixteen, recovering from those endless nights of shrieking
across the house, out into the yard and
into the cold moonlight to wish myself into some
other species; the endless silent Stooges' bangs and thwacks,
some self-preservation up against inherited solitude;
bent almost in half, the copper piping of my family grief
that always raked itself across me
until I was deformed by it,
until I was defined by it—
but dammit,

          I hope that girl's doing well.
I hope she can keep down food

and it's nourishing her. I hope her cells are cheering
like parents in the stands at a game, even if those men still exist—
important men, I imagine. Men who now run conglomerates
and have well-to-do families. Or maybe men I see
every day at work. Or whose books I read.

And how am I here? With my life intact?
I'm painful to the touch only when I don't light
a candle and praise oblivion, give myself over
to nothingness—and is it every day
or was it long ago,
that I'd slid shut my teenage self's veranda doors
and stepped
onto the world's fancy balconies
and was prepared to do something drastic
like live and live and live.

Letter to a Letter to the Editors

> She clearly knew her melodramatic fears were
> groundless, and avoided challenge by expressing
> her invective through poetry—a multifaceted,
> intentionally cryptic medium through which she
> could conveniently deny unprovoked attacks upon
> those who loved her.
>
> —Anne Sexton's nieces, Lisa Taylor Tompson
> and Mary Gray Ford, in a letter to the editor,
> "Anne Sexton's Vision of Reality," *New York Times*,
> August 1991, after the publication of Diane Wood
> Middlebrook's *Anne Sexton: A Biography*

> Tell all the Truth but tell it slant—
>
> —Emily Dickinson

Where Blanche saw reindeer on the roof, Santa, and
expressions of love, Anne saw a particularly villainous season.
Anne could "find a cloud in the sunniest sky." These people
from Scituate, Mass.—I know them in my head and heart.
The way they say how it is interesting but not surprising,
that everyone who is slaughtered (reputation-wise) is dead.
The way one person took up so much static-electric space,
and spread out. How could that sweet old man we loved
have molested her? they ask. (Oh that's how predators work,
separating one from the rest.) The body cringing at the sight
of the one who harmed it—the deep voice of it comes out, to
balance the well-meaning upper-middle-class, the cherished,

the sweet, loving facade. Nothing is accurate. Nothing is right. And who would see clots of blood for beautiful roses? (They ask.) Presuming the wet, real grass is just yours, the garden where everything is flourishing, the sidewalk where a chicken bone lies, the way the morning takes its time to unwrap, and the street begins to fill like a play—nothing you lay your eyes upon is just yours. And it is also all yours.

*

Does anguish only come from within your own head? Yes.
    But so does the meaning of words, the depiction of a
    cloudless sky, where there is nothing, no sky at all,
only an unbroken stream of water hoarded in it. And Anne
    went and ruined everything with her fucking chemical
    imbalance! Her strange and unsettled anger! Her
    "insistence on what she saw as brutal honesty"!

What is "brutal honesty" in poetry? How does that work?

Of course she chose a mysterious medium to talk about a
    cloud that existed in a sunny sky. The "pleasant memories
    were slashed." ☹ They assume that Anne assumed that
    poems were concerned with fact. But she knew the
    complicated presentation of existence. She didn't write

essays or memoir. She was all "imagination, without basis in fact." Is imagination constrained by fact? The accepted social story must be consistent. The story must be sanctioned. The story must be liked. Must not upset great-aunts, carted off, screaming. Awe at death was what she had in the end. Sisters will hate one another, and nieces will always take their mother's side. So normal, I know! My family is full of angry sisters who want to explain their childhoods in different ways.

*

I had a vision last night of a massive heron with a shimmering rainbow neck that stood, in my mother's backyard, on top of a machine that dug graves. And the heron's chicks were gathered under her wings as the machine swayed and clanged; the man at the levers, indifferent in his control center, continued to dig where the birds had lived—"But they are rare!" I cried up to him. "RARE! LIKE, 'NOT SEEN NORMALLY!'" But he continued on, saying *he* didn't think they were rare. And I watched, there being nothing I could do about it.

What unwarranted conclusions can we draw? What can horror provide? There was also the "accident of birth" hypothesis offered by Anne's nieces.

Is it "a misfitted chromosome," a "genetic misfortune," that makes a poet?

> "Some families, confronted with a child like Anne, would have turned her over to state agencies for warehousing.
> Our family chose to accept responsibility for one of our own."

—this, this medium is not done with itself. And I'll take her babble, her immature, completely unwarranted conclusions. And tell things honestly with a slant like a roof where apples roll down, and snow slides off, under which phoebes make weird hive nests and lay eggs—I think a poet will see truth through a distorted reverence for the underlying truth of shadows; "human decency" has nothing to do with poems—

And where do these poems' truths come from? We are
mistaken when we try to make broken things new; rather,
we must proceed through the outrageous, cryptic medium
of vision, which is only curiosity at being alive. When one
has seen horrors in the midst of everyone's enjoyment,
to pretend to see reindeer and elves is to ignore a more
powerful perception, covering it with a sheet, as over a
wound that will fester. The ordinary conceptual system
that we live by is governed by metaphors neither obvious
to nor desired by most citizens. The automation of
living is comforting. To closely examine the realities
of germs, for instance, disgusts people, drives them to
enthusiastically kill the vital bacteria necessary for a
healthy organism. Purell™ and a set of agreed-upon
concepts. It wasn't that Anne was bad, just that, for
whatever reason, she wasn't let in on the agreed-upon
system of understanding reality—and her madness was
stayed a little with poetry.

So, dearest nieces of Anne Sexton, *I get it*. But I disagree.

The Green Word

In a dream my twin brother was telling me a word
for the sudden appearance of green—when, in spring,
it comes, exploding from branches the way college boys explode
out the doors of their frat house onto the cool, wet grass
    at dawn. He was telling me how this was the key to
    understanding human suffering. This one word, which,
he said from the floor, he had to tell people about, his turned-up
    face perspiring from his earnest emphasis on this point;
and he looked just like he did when we were nineteen years
    old and backpacking in Italy. It was so hot and humid in
    Florence we couldn't sleep.
Terrible nights on hostel bunk beds visited by a little old woman
who would come in with linen piled in her arms
and point her finger angrily at my boots on the bed.
I had no taste for wine then, no feel for maps. I was always
    stopping
and staring for too long at sculptures,
which were everywhere—I didn't even have to know where I
    was going,
they came to me, those statues—men with their swords up in
    the air
and severed heads in their hands, women with small perfect
    gray breasts—
and my brother would disappear into the crowded streets
as if he'd lived there for decades and was late to work.

It would take me all day to find my way back to him. I had
    no sense of direction,
no grasp of etiquette. I loaded film in our camera, gave both
    of us haircuts.
He was already becoming older than me,
the towers had just fallen, and he'd watched from his dorm
    rooftop, his faculties
slowly guillotining, slamming shut, and—where was that
    word then?
That word for when the green comes like Swamp Thing
when he hallucinates himself across the bayou in torn
    ligatures of moss
and plant matter, transforming his intellectual pain
into carbon-based superpowers?
Now, on the weekends my brother and I get together on the
    internet.
We talk about the importance of nonbeing, of reactions.
When I think too much, I think the words "everything is as it
    should be," very loudly.
He works at a hospital answering phones and directing people;
he meditates every morning;
I visit him in Portland

and he meets me at the airport, even though I can get to him
    on my own now, and he always comes with a sandwich and
    iced tea,
and he shows me gateways on his smart phone and the best places
to watch birds. His wife comes back from work and uncovers a
    book on souls
and lights sage. There's a poster of the body's flailing chakras
    facing you
when you sit down on the toilet; and my brother and I walk
    and walk and walk, endlessly through Portland's parks, and
    long streets going nowhere in particular
but the general direction of water—
the smell of it hits you first, acrid and mossy.
And I still walk too slow to keep up with him;
I still walk with a clinical leisureliness. I feel
like Mom's Subaru that is always breaking down.
I feel like we're a couple of human sandbags at a levee,
like we're lying down together
at the base of a shuddering dam.

Migration

This time of year the birds fly in elegant mobs,
tragic and sinister against gathering clouds.
It always made me sad to see the one trailing at the end, who I
     thought was
falling behind, tripping like a head of a musical note;
dark dots making swirls over and around the obscene billboards,
gathering in the empty trees like relentless matching ornaments—
no distinction between them from this distance,
their eyes kept from me, their hearts blue-red compasses
leading to Florida—
I watch them like a child might watch a father love
another child better—they smash into commuter planes or into
     a sky-blue tower
(the greatest trick of humans, making the sky into matter—),
those little feathery dinosaurs stopping at the mall ponds
to drink, calling to one another, sensing the change
in the wind, working as a team—it makes me want
to get stoned on the front steps, lit from within—seeing
these migrating jewels, elegant survivors, feathered delicacies,
musical geniuses, flinging themselves like a ballerina
made of smaller ballerinas;
these small dwindling barrettes of Nature—
there's simply nothing more important than them making it.
I want to haul my mattress onto the roof.
I want to compare them to the stars, to light, to pepper.

I want to follow them. Want to do something
other than take this exit off the freeway
and leave them in my rearview mirror:
fumbling clear black angels, backup dancers, flawless
     cheerleading squad
from some more transcendent universe
piling up on one another, perfectly—swallowing the sky like
     a silk scarf,
above, silent, powerful, better than me, in every way,
hustling over the shipwrecked world.

Retreating Knights and Riderless Horses, *or* Poem with Another Poem Halfway Through It

I keep a box of illegal paraphernalia on my table. I keep a knife
in a pet rock. I hire men to come to try to remove it.
The one who does will be king of my life. I keep my life
right here by my other life. My other life keeps to itself.
I have two guitars. One expensive dress. Too many lamps. I
    take myself
very seriously. My name is permanent. I cut a hole in the wall
and watch the neighbor watching TV. It's not even
sexy. Cracking open a bottle with my bottle of pills
prescribed forever like sunlight.
I'm going to a new restaurant in town
to lay waste
to its reputation.

*

Halfway through the poem another poem took over.
The two poems fought. It was
a bloody battle that lasted seven hundred years.
Big choices were made
and gods among men died.
While stained sheets were wrung out in the wind,
cannons roared.

After seven hundred years the two poems were mangled.
They couldn't tell the difference anymore between themselves.
And they became, then, masochistic:
self-inflicting
on the battlefield their rage.
On a glorious morning, high up on a hill,
in hussar boots and mauve silk vest, the poem raged on—
infantry in massed columns—
the trillium of chivalry
ridden to its final thing.
It wore itself
into a bonfire, dying down. You have
to stand very close to it
with your hands or ass
even closer.
In the dark it's like porn,
beet red
and bright orange, flecks of engorged blue veins,
humping in the ash
for eternity.

The Fall

If it happened at all
it was the apes who won,
shimmering stark-naked
and sitting a little apart from Adam,
who was deep into his clothing
the cuff links and soft leather,
pulling the zipper up Eve's back
and she, clasping the bra shut like a jewelry box—

What to do with this mind?
Throw everything
into the fire and scream
into the internet
that there's nothing to do
but stand in the dark recesses
throwing a bright red dodge ball
against the bone facade
and fall in and out of love
with suffering?

The Woman Downstairs

In the night I realize we're living in the same apartment building.
All this time! She lives downstairs, in a room filled with cats.
I rush to her—my grandmother, in a total chaos of furniture,
lying on a mattress on the floor.
"No one comes by anymore," she says. "I'm so bored."
In her face I can see the unfathomable loneliness
of the dead, like its own failed revolution.
Her body spilling out of a flannel button-down shirt.
Her wrinkled skin pooled
beneath her half-naked body.
The smell of urine is overwhelming.
Different parts of the vacuum cleaner are scattered around
like sniper rifle fittings, fancy small attachments
piled up around the mattress: Sub 20 Universal Brush,
Mini Turbo, the Extra Wide Upholstery sucker—
which I begin to gather and click together—what good is any
    of it?
"Oh, don't clean," she begs from the floor.

The Walking Dead

She doesn't know she's dead, so you don't bring it up.
In the woods you carry her around with your bow and arrow.
She's so thin, her skin is like a bolt of peach-flecked silk
sagging off the arm. Her hair is unnatural, fiery red.
A bird is trapped in the living room—"Darn thing came down
    from the chimney, covered in soot," you say.

It gets bigger and bigger until it's a massive red-black blur
flapping in your face.

The Lit Club Slaughter

Lost in the coatroom at the Gramercy lit club,
in my sister's dress, feeling the pockets
of famous writers, living and dead—their brittle balls
of used Kleenex, their grocery lists
and fragrant marijuana in tins, their loose change
and half-done cough drops, cracked cellphones
and hair brushes, their Mactaggart jewelry—holy
amethyst and gold Egyptian talisman,
their nips of Old Crow, letters of intent,
trust documents and set lists—I'm too drunk
to bargain. Instead, I'm hounding Patti Smith about her life.
That punk-poet genius—I'm telling her about you.
I'm making things up. It was
a beautiful, caramel-colored evening, until I was
slashing my wrists in the bathroom
with a pair of scissors after I'd been led by Rosanne
into the street and put into a cab.
And I reached your voice
across the veil. It said: *quit smoking.*
You're getting fat.
Be nice to your mother.
In general, I am the life
of the party. And it's always the eve of battle.
In general, I am hard and quiet. Like a floorboard

from a tree long gone. Like a floorboard
sanded down, shellacked, hammered in a house
no one lives in anymore.

In the Champagne Room with Grandma

Where are the high rollers in the MSCOG?
Tens and hundreds of thousands of dollars for a single visit,
the hardest part of loving her.
The water is deep. Too deep to touch
the bottom; I have to swim around the rim of the glass
holding on. Mourning doves in the chandeliers,
with delicate clucks, gold lamé and plush control room,
old lady without her pants on,
incontinent beauty queen,
peering out of a beaded curtain
or lying back, reading Wodehouse on a black pleather couch
chuckling in the yellow lightbulb spray—

we have your best interests at heart.
We take you into the Champagne Room, blushing,
looking lost and easy at the entrance to the peep show.
Are you paying attention?
We're way down on the food chain with the krill.
And we're the only species left alone to die in bed.

The shadow grows long in the club.
Swim into her, who hangs in your family tree,
the plum tree that won't bear fruit.
Drag the lake. Keep it coming.
There are no limits.
Premium content: Sappho, the essential Philip K. Dick,
dead leaves around a daffodil
too early to pick;
coffee before dawn, rye bread with I Can't Believe It's Not Butter!
everything tastes so real—
maple leaves made of silver;
we turn to swans,
we wear black mourning brassieres—

Here, in the MSCOG, we love you just as you are.
We pay your tuition.
We overdraft for you.
We write you check after check—for food,
or a cord of wood, new paintbrushes—
we'll pay for it, while we say, "I'm BROKE. I haven't *GOT* it!"
But we got it. We always got it.

Elegy with Clothes

All of your giant beige bras
floated up into the atmosphere.
Blue eggs fell down the chimney;
the porch,
losing its screened-in mind,
caved in.
I mistake one living cell for another.
Hand on the mallet
of my life—
you come
detonating midair
with your own grief—
it's not even mine.

I watch mice eat through everything,
their droppings
like beads of hashish.
The world begins as
a wolf tied to a flower.
Can you see how it happens
like that?
Something too violent
is attached to something
too living?

I'll Be Happy

once I am able to plunge, pig head on the platter that I am,
into the next jazz era of my sense. When the moon floats into me,
and the teetotaler mountain range—when the moon,
with its neon disk mouth, liquors up, gets wasted, wide open
on the human-achievement anecdotes, when the corn
gets more terrifying than me, in my maternity nightgowns,
and the rain leaves everything in the RV husked with dew
and the night sends out its bizarre night-bird sounds—
once I am freed from my education, held aloft by my ignorance
and the auspices of my wasted afternoons—
well then—*what then?* Then I will make a new list
and long for happiness again.

Historic Flaws

I am going back to the mountains
where the alternating universe of autumn
descends over you in an erotic squat. Out of that blank
and meaningless Play-Doh of my psychic flesh
I am moving on. I am a pupil of fading antiquity.
Sprawled across the table, in a lament about health care
and the ineptitude of the System.
Nothing burns quite like the System. It comes at you
when you ask for help, displaying its super-talons
around a clutch of arrows, saying *No*.

"What deeds could man ever have done
if he had not been enveloped in the dust-cloud
of the unhistorical?" Nietzsche asks this morning
from a small pamphlet on my lap, issued in 1949
in New York City, which I am leaving now,
like a wife from her distant husband
who will not stop to ask her why she is weeping
while on the floor of the closet she slices apart his silk ties.

The Dark Ages, Revisited

Up early again reading Geneviève Fraisse's *Reason's Muse:*
    Sexual Difference and the Birth of Democracy—
in which I read the line

"A man satisfied with prejudices is not concerned
by the disorder of his arguments."
Which illuminates Donald Trump, who oils his way across the
    tangible world.

But what about the Möbius Strip Club of Grief?
I find there's no solace in it for me today.
I feel the phantom limbs of my predecessors
waving in the air. I feel
a public vs. private activity of self-mutilation: the human race
voting for the wrong thing.
And to exercise our rights, to fulfill our duties—our education
    seems, today,
to have not been enough.

And, well, women have long differed from men, in their (let's
    call it) *social destinies*
but not in their capabilities.
It has come again, the Dark Ages,
arguing for factory jobs and the security of middle management.
The hallucination far from actual benevolence of the
    universe.
The life lived for someone else, for a few free months of
    leisure before
expensive death.

My second thesis might involve *Love*, and/or the "Fine Mind."
Because the woman's mind is different. Invoked differently,
    even as her body is—
I'm not sure of my argument yet.
(It was always my weakest skill   in school, knowing my
    argument.)

But, as a whole, reader, it is faulty

to speak of "sex and sexuality when it is the mind at issue."
So why am I writing this psychosexual opus to the mind of
    my women?

And Hillary Clinton, what are you doing right now?
(The club is closed for the week, ran out of solace.

The smell
of bleach in the air.
I keep replaying it in my head—)
On some level, weakness and strength
have nothing to do with the physical form. But this relationship

between the physical and the intellectual forms—
what of that? Leaving behind the imposed moral activities
of the human mind—we must invent, while living a life:

nothing irrelevant here, nothing stopping you—*invent!*

invent!
invent!

stretch out
a social destiny!

       (—I keep saying this to my mother, to my
    sister, to the old impression of Grandma
brushing her hair upside down
and reading the encyclopedia in a flowerbed—)

Invent with your hands! or forever hold your peace!

But it is pointless to tell you how I
feel. Often we don't *feel* like doing anything.
Each shred of dignity is shredded again. And it looks just like it is:
like high school football all over again, framed in my window,
    running hard
to get one more yard line ahead, on only a few feet of rubber grass.

The dream of multiple selves that keeps not coming true
is made true with a few feelings, set aside.
The apartment we're in is strange and small.
My things don't fit. I destroy my things.
I sneak them to the trashcan. I feel
awful. I'd meant
to do something.
But what good is any of it?
I let it go
sometimes—this grief.

Goodbye, I say. *Thank you for your service*, I say.
Old heliumed balloon wheezing out,
hovering five feet in the air

just like the ghost that can neither ascend nor
fall. Stuck in the ether. Sweeping. Wiping everything down.
   Locking
the front door. Turning off lights. Sitting, finally,
sighing, saying to the dark
bittersweet self: *Thank you. Oh, Thank you.*

Thank you.

And Goodnight.

Bibliography:

Mason, Ameria Ruth Gere. *The Women of the French Salons.*
New York: The Century Company, 1891.

Stone, Ruth. "The Möbius Strip of Grief," *What Love Comes To.*
Port Townsend: Copper Canyon Press, 2008.

Stevenson, Robert Louis. "At the Sea-Side," *The Golden Book of
Poetry. Ed. Jane Werner Watson; Gertrude E Espenscheid.* New York:
Simon and Schuster, 1947.

Fraisse, Geneviève. *Reason's Muse: Sexual Difference and the Birth of
Democracy.* Translated by Jane Marie Todd. Chicago: University of
Chicago Press, 1994.

(Page 31, the poem ends with the famous ending line from the
poem *Le Mérite des Femmes* as was referenced in *Reason's Muse:
Sexual Difference and the Birth of Democracy.*)

Dick, Philip K. *VALIS.* New York: Bantam Books, 1981.

Mann, Bonnie. *Women's Liberation and the Sublime: Feminism,
Postmodernism, Environment.* Oxford University Press, 2006.

Magazines in which these poems have previously appeared:

"[Odin plucked out his eye in exchange for a drink]," and "How Not," in *Stedt*; "Lap Dance," in *The Georgia Review*; "Letter to a Letter to the Editors," "Math," and "Emily Dickinson," in *The Brooklyn Rail*; "Apes," "Introduction," "Hunter," and "Interior Design," in *Tin House*; "The Ones Who Got Away With It," in *Pinwheel*; "Historic Flaws," and "Making Applesauce with My Dead Grandmother," at *poets.org*; "Migration," Visionary Binary; "Self-Destruction Sequence," and "The Fates," in *jubilat*; "Elegy with a Swear Word," and "Elegy With Clothes," in *The Bakery*.